T0132134

Turning Points:

Changing Lives One Event at a Time

Co-edited by Paulette Costa and Lois Arsenault
Foreword by Mike Staver, CEO The Staver Group

authorHOUSE®

AuthorHouse™
1663 Liberty Drive
Bloomington, IN 47403
www.authorhouse.com
Phone: 1-800-839-8640

©2012 by Paulette Costa - New Life Essentials LLC

No part of this book may be reproduced, stored in
a retrieval system, or transmitted by any means
without the written permission of the author.

Published by AuthorHouse   12/30/2011

ISBN: 978-1-4685-2803-9 (sc)
ISBN: 978-1-4685-2802-2 (e)

Library of Congress Control Number: 2011962652

Any people depicted in stock imagery provided by Thinkstock are models,
and such images are being used for illustrative purposes only.
Certain stock imagery © Thinkstock.

This book is printed on acid-free paper.

Because of the dynamic nature of the Internet, any web addresses or
links contained in this book may have changed since publication and
may no longer be valid. The views expressed in this work are solely those
of the author and do not necessarily reflect the views of the publisher,
and the publisher hereby disclaims any responsibility for them.

Table of Contents

Introduction

Turning points are part and parcel of the landscape traveled by every human being during their life journey. How each of us experiences those moments, how we process them, and what we do with them is another matter, indeed.

Turning points do not define who we are. Rather, they are those times, those experiences, which are sufficiently impactful as to inform how we behave in given situations. A turning point carries enormous potential to precipitate life-altering decisions. Such a moment may ignite a fire of change in the way we live and work in our world; the world as we see it, individually.

Turning Points: Changing Lives One Event at a Time is a collection of vignettes from every-day people who experienced events that forever changed their lives. These experiences and their outcomes didn't gain national media attention yet were personally extraordinary ... the result of stepping out of comfort zones and trusting one's heart and our gut; of knowing nothing will change if we don't change our *self*.

Dedication

To our contributors:

Each of you is an inspiration and we honor you for your commitment to the *Turning Points* project. You have openly shared pieces of your lives as an invitation for readers to acknowledge defining moments that could change theirs. We are grateful for your willingness and courage to write your stories so that others may learn and benefit from your experiences, the realizations they brought, the changes you made, and the ultimate outcome of personal growth.

"Every human has four endowments - self awareness, conscience, independent will and creative imagination. These give us the ultimate human freedom ... the power to choose, to respond, to change."

Stephen Covey

Foreword

Mike Staver

If there was ever a time when a book's time had come this is it. I can't think of a more relevant and timely topic than *Turning Points*. We live in unprecedented times of change. Each day we are challenged with events that can have significant impact on our lives. For some those events are inconsequential, for others, significant and even heart-wrenching life change is experienced.

Some life events require courage, others resolve and still others require quiet contemplation. But most important are the events that actually change the course of your life. Those are the events and life experiences that are turning points. In my own life my turning points have come at the most unexpected times with the most unexpected results.

Think through your life, through the experiences you have had and I will guess you won't have to think very long before you can identify your own turning points.

Whether it came from tragedy, luck, serendipity, life circumstances or any other cause one thing is for sure, it was powerful enough to change the way you think, or act, or love or work. It was significant enough for you to evaluate, reconsider or change something significant. A turning point has impact at our core. It's not always immediate but it is always significant. In our coaching practice it has been interesting to note that turning points are deeply personal. The events that have significant impact in one person's life may not even be noticed in another person's.

The perspective of those observing our lives is not nearly as critical as what happens from YOUR perspective! As you read this powerful work you will read stories. But if you really want to experience this book I challenge you to work to be *with* the story you are reading. "Be with it" means to walk the path with the author. Allow yourself to fully experience how your own turning points have created the you who is reading this page right now.

If you are a person who needs a change in your life, I want you to know that a turning point is just ahead for you. Don't let it pass you by. Be aware, be in tune and honor it when it comes. One of the dangers we humans face is the belief our birthright is to feel comfortable. For the time you spend reading this book I would like to suggest you suspend that belief. Allow yourself to accept the fact that the discomfort we experience often leads to transformation.

The journey is not always what we had planned or hoped but it is the journey we find ourselves on and so we have choices. I was recently watching an athlete interviewed on ESPN about his life. He spoke of being given up for adoption at nine years old and of the horrible experiences he had. It was difficult to listen to him, until he said something that hit me like a bolt of lightning. He told of an experience when his high school principal and guidance counselor brought him into the office and they were crying because of a stupid decision he had made. The athlete being interviewed said, "At that moment I knew two things: people cared about me and I had a choice. I could turn to the bad or I could turn to the good. Thankfully I turned to the good." Today he is one of the most celebrated running backs in the NFL. That was a turning point. We have choices and those choices determine our individual destinies.

Come from a place of abundance and gratitude as you celebrate with those whose stories you will read here. May they comfort, inspire, and encourage you! Remember, you have choices and people care about you!

Mike Staver is the CEO of The Staver Group. Together with his colleagues of professional development consultants, he provides keynote presentations, consulting programs and workshops. He also conducts executive coaching sessions that help people lead with courage and authenticity. Mike is a confidential advisor to Fortune 500 CEOs and executives, a nationally recognized expert in crisis control and a published author.

"Change does not roll in on the wheels of inevitability, but comes through continuous struggle. And so we must straighten our backs and work for our freedom. A man can't ride you unless your back is bent."

Martin Luther King, Jr.

Leaning Into the Curves - "Allowing"

Lois Arsenault

Among my favorite motorcycle rides are those with lots of curves. Those routes are more challenging than the long straight roads, especially when punctuated with a few hills. Riding the curves requires just the right touch, attention, and confidence in me, the bike, and the universe.

Approaching a curve, I take a moment to slow down slightly to check it out. Then, I accelerate and lean the bike into the curve, keeping my eye on where I want to go. I am confident in my bike and my ability to almost effortlessly maintain control if I just keep my eyes looking ahead and my bike leaned just enough to hug the road. Once I complete all the necessary actions, allowing the bike and laws of nature to take me around the curve becomes the most joyful part of the experience.

I've learned to lean into rather than fight the curves

1

in my life's path as well. Sustaining hyper-vigilance and negativity requires much more energy than I am willing to devote to conflict. I'd rather ride the curve and allow whatever new experience awaits me around the bend. My case in point:

Recently, through the technology of online introductions, a very special gentleman showed up in my life. Attraction was immediate. I questioned myself. "What will happen if I just be myself and 'allow' the universe to take over? Will he go away? Will I be left wondering what could have been if I'd only been a bit more persistent?" Old habits die slowly and sometimes linger on with great tenacity. Still, I "allowed."

As a result of allowing myself to ride the curve of this new beginning, I am blessed daily with fresh insight into just how special this man is. Perfect? Not by a long shot but then, neither am I. Who wants perfect?

As a result of allowing, I am perpetually grateful for the joy of celebrating our individuality and imperfections as qualities to keep our lives new and interesting.

As a result of allowing, I feel no need to change who either of us is.

As a result of allowing, the need for control is diminished and the joys of life are much more readily available to me.

All that life has to offer is in the here and now, at any age and stage, if we will but "allow" the universe to put the treasure in our path when we are ready to appreciate its true value.

It is during our darkest moments that we must focus to see the light.

Aristotle Onassis

Always another One around the Corner
Lois Arsenault

In the summer of 1993, a health club acquaintance showed me a picture of her completing her first triathlon. In silence I thought, *I want that look on my face.* Eventually I asked my health club friend about the training regimen. Not only did she describe the training but introduced me to other tri-athletes and a newly formed triathlon club. It came down to accepting the challenge or passing on the opportunity and forever wondering "what if?"

Throughout the next winter and spring, along with my friend and new triathlon buddies, I learned the right way to swim, learned about interval training, brick training, the value of long slow runs, and the joy of gravity while biking on the downhill. The training challenged my body more than anything I had ever attempted before in my life. In June of 1994 I completed my first triathlon at the age of forty-three. I have a picture of myself running over the finish line and when I look at that picture I remember what I learned from training and completing that first race. I knew, without doubt, if I could do that, I could do anything.

The sense of self-confidence I discovered around the corner following my first triathlon is still with me and stronger than ever at age sixty. Around the bend, holding hands with my newly heightened confidence was a treasured friendship that grew out of many hours of training together ... countless laps in the pool, lake swims, long runs, long bike rides and long talks along the way. That relationship has grown stronger every year hence.

When the time came to decide about a graduate program, I knew I could do it, all the while taking on a new and rather large professional move upward to a very demanding executive position. The work required of me to complete the degree program helped build confidence in my writing and planted the seed of a book I am writing about my philosophy for caring for those diagnosed with Alzheimer's disease. I am certain the book will be published, along with another two pieces of work I wrote years ago. I know I can do it.

Confidence building is cumulative. Each of the corners I have turned in my life proved to result in a new confidence and a new sense of myself and my place in this world. Each turning point added the texture of experience and the richness of people from diverse backgrounds. As for me, I welcome the winding road, changes in direction, and bumps in a journey filled with turning points over the easy ride on a straight open road.

"Always continue the climb. It is possible for you to do whatever you choose, if you first get to know who you are and are willing to work with a power that is greater than ourselves to do it."

Ella Wheeler Wilcox

Saying *IT* Out Loud

Lois Arsenault

Two years ago, I knew the time had come for me to make an important decision necessary for my own wellbeing. I had not taken any action on my decision but rather kept turning it over and over in my head, not moving forward. Have you ever found yourself doing the same thing? Everything changed when I very off-handedly commented to my dearest friend that I was certain my marriage was, for all intents and purposes, over. Within less than a year, I was living in my own space and healing from my self-inflicted journey into the world of negativity and joyless existence.

Take a minute to think about a time when thoughts of a need for change bobbed around in your head, in perpetual percolation, so to speak. Decisions, as with coffee, need time to grow bolder, attaining distinctive characteristics. When the time is right, we turn off the percolator and enjoy the results of the real deal.

When we have a necessary decision to make or action to take, if we will but say "it" out loud, the "it" becomes real. Saying "it" out loud liberates the thought, puts "it" out into the universe, and makes us accountable.

Once I related my thought, my need for a decision, to a dear friend in the course of casual conversation, I moved forward.

What will you do the next time your decisions are in perpetual percolation?

If

If you can keep your head when all about you
Are losing theirs and blaming it on you;
If you can trust yourself when all men doubt you,
But make allowance for their doubting too;
If you can wait and not be tired by waiting,
Or, being lied about, don't deal in lies,
Or, being hated, don't give way to hating,
And yet don't look too good, nor talk too wise;
If you can dream - and not make dreams your master;
If you can think - and not make thoughts your aim;
If you can meet with triumph and disaster
And treat those two imposters just the same;
If you can bear to hear the truth you've spoken
Twisted by knaves to make a trap for fools,
Or watch the things you gave your life to broken,
And stoop and build 'em up with wornout tools;
If you can make one heap of all your winnings
And risk it on one turn of pitch-and-toss,
And lose, and start again at your beginnings
And never breath a word about your loss;
If you can force your heart and nerve and sinew
To serve your turn long after they are gone,
And so hold on when there is nothing in you
Except the Will which says to them: "Hold on";
If you can talk with crowds and keep your virtue,
Or walk with kings - nor lose the common touch;
If neither foes nor loving friends can hurt you;
If all men count with you, but none too much;
If you can fill the unforgiving minute
With sixty seconds' worth of distance run -
Yours is the Earth and everything that's in it,
And - which is more - you'll be a Man my son!
Rudyard Kipling

Lois R. Arsenault, M.Ed.

Lois is sole proprietor of 4 Rivers Connections, a business dedicated to helping individuals rediscover their true identity, at the core. She lives with her little rescue dog, Spike, and is the proud mom of two adult children. In her spare time Lois enjoys singing, mostly folk songs, and playing her guitar.

For twenty-eight years Lois has served fragile older adults in numerous settings; skilled nursing centers, assisted living residences, and most recently in an adult day health center. Dignity and quality of life for those individuals are her primary goals in whatever venue she serves. She takes time to learn who each person is, at their core, and approaches their care from that perspective.

Lois has written a professional manual designed to facilitate reminiscence and language skills among elders experiencing memory impairments through the use of creative writing. Currently she is working on a book that describes the importance of Core Centered Care[SM] for memory-impaired adults. This work outlines the principles and methods for care that begins with an individual's core identity. The book is intended for professionals and family caregivers alike.

Life in Lois' world is never static. A consummate seeker, she continues introspection to remain in touch with her own personal "core." Her individual discoveries are never wasted and often put to use in her writing as well as in the creation of unique jewelry and other one-of-a-kind art pieces.

Learn more about Lois' world and become a 4 Rivers Connections fan on Facebook at the 4 Rivers Connections page.

"Man never made any material as resilient as the human spirit."

Bern Williams

Sacrifice and Swans
Christina M. Cody

I knew the day would come. Six months away from my husband, my best friend, was one aspect of being a Navy wife that I had been dreading since November.

The months passed too quickly; the days, even faster. Each day I yearned for the sun not to raise the next. I wished upon stars, and I wanted to lasso the moon, so that I might freeze moments of tenderness, of laughter, of him. There were mornings I would watch Daniel sleep and catch myself caressing his cheeks trying desperately to sear into my memory the shape of his nose, the softness of his lips, and the curve of his eyelashes.

And then I took a deep breath, and June twenty-first arrived. The alarm clock sounded with the local country music station. Daniel, my love, was sleeping peacefully, and I would wake him for the last time in six months. Watching him breathe and dream, I rested my cheek on his chest, counting heartbeats…babum, babum, babum.

He woke and we laced our fingers into their comfortable places.

We talked. We were quiet. We just were.

With each new song finding its way into our moments, we reluctantly realized the day was whispering our names. Begrudgingly, we slid our legs over the side of the bed to feel the coolness of the wood floor beneath our feet, and we began to ready ourselves for the day. The carport door clicked behind us and the car cranked just fine, much to my dismay. As we drove the short distance to the sub base, we listened to music, held hands tenderly, and spoke briefly of how the next six months would be long.

Looming there on pier thirty-three was Daniel's new home, an enormous black tube of steel and diesel fuel only twenty feet away, mocking the tears I held at bay.

Other wives were on the verge of convulsions, crying, sobbing into their husband's shoulders, leaving salt traces of breaking hearts. No, I would never let Daniel see me cry like that on his departure. I wanted him to remember me smiling when he walked down the pier; I was stubborn and forced the lump in my throat to retreat.

Feeling the moments slip away, we discussed how the clouds were beginning to form and how the sky was my favorite color of cornflower blue. Among the submarines swam two white swans that seemed to always be present when Daniel was leaving or returning home from sea. They swam, more like glided, over the little ripples in the water. Hearts were breaking, tears were flowing, and the world's beauty surrounded them as on any other day.

Time tapped our shoulders, so we began saying our last goodbyes. Here it was, eight thirty a.m. and we were embracing and expressing how we already missed each other.

Daniel turned to walk to the hunk of metal that I hoped would protect him. I slid into the driver's seat and watched him trudge down the pier with his green sea bag slung over his left shoulder. I glanced once more at the swans knowing that days of solitude and empty moments were beginning. Driving away and out of Daniel's vision, the lump in my throat was victorious and the tears of a lifetime streamed down my cheek.

Now, more than twelve years have passed and Daniel has been out to sea more months than I care to count. I still watch him breathe, we still hold hands tenderly, and we still share quiet moments together but, most importantly, two swans still swim in my memory reminding me of my strength, my turning point as a Navy wife, and that, somewhere in the world, there is another wife choking back tears so her husband will remember her smile.

"There is no telling how far you will have to run while chasing a dream."

Unknown

The Gardener's War
Christina M. Cody

Have you ever heard, "People get wiser with age?" Well I have and I am of the "age" to be wise because I have learned over the years that one way we become wiser is because of little battles, little every day menial tasks that test us. For instance, fighting with clothes dryer vents that continually become clogged, so you think little beings live in the vents to collect all the lint into one place and not let it escape, or telling your children to, "Be nice to one another for two minutes!," when they have just walked into the room aggravating each other, or planting flowers. Yes, I said it, "Planting flowers!"

My knees ache. I kneel on the cool fall grass bending over my flowerbed. Attempting to beat the high noon sun, I have been digging holes two inches deep and three inches apart for many morning hours. One by one I drop bulb after bulb into the ground and cover them with mound after mound of soil with hope of seeing bright red tulips and blue hyacinths in the spring.

On my forehead, sweat begins to bead in droves occasionally falling into the freshly dug holes. Can it be considered the first watering? I continue to dig hole after hole only to find platoons of New England rocks standing guard protecting their soil. One by one I pluck them from their bunkers and shake my head at the growing pile of soldiers scowling at my nerve, my determination to complete the task of bombarding their land.

Just when I feel the war is turning in my direction, the sun's midday fire begins to reinforce the soldiers from the invading tulip bulbs and my callused hands. He stalks my hunched back with his rays of destruction, laughing at my efforts to protect my fair skin from his invasion. "Sunscreen. Sunscreen!" my skin orders. To this, he snickers menacingly and slowly creeps in from the trees' shadows, all the while burning my neck and stinging my arms.

A gardener knows when to retreat, so I gather the remaining bulbs, stand to feel my knees complain, and look up to the bright sun who shouts his victory cry in my direction. You may have won this battle Mr. Sun, but the morning is my ally.

"Never too old, never too bad, never too late, never too sick to start from scratch once again."

Bikram Choudhury.

Christina M. Cody

While growing up in Alabama, I spent weekends in the library with my mother devouring books and gaining the sense that I should tell stories. Currently, I have published two children's books: *The Perfectly Imperfect Pumpkin* and *The Pirate Scope*. Although being an author is what keeps me sane, being a proud Navy wife and a mother to two wonderful, yet zany, children are still the best adventure ever! www.christinacody.org.

"I read to discover other authors and the worlds they share.

I write to discover the author within me and all that I can share with the world." C.Cody

"If we don't change, we don't grow. If we don't grow, we aren't really living."

Gail Sheehy

When Dreams Come True
Paulette Costa

June, 2007 - I was writing my first novel and with the support and encouragement of my loving partner, a fair retirement savings, and lots of chutzpah, I grabbed the brass ring. I left Connecticut, my home for more than twenty years and my sweet condo just a mile south of Hole-In-The-Wall Beach in Niantic Bay, and we moved to Florida's Treasure Coast where I would retire from the drone of a corporate career and pursue my passion for writing.

Every day in Florida was another day in paradise. When I wasn't writing, I was snorkeling, enjoying time with friends, resting on the beach, and being a tourist. One of my favorite sights, if you could call it a sight, was the Florida sky. It's bigger than any I've ever seen – so vast, with a sun so bright, it heats the earth from the moment it rises until a blanket of stars takes over as the day comes to a close.

Nine months passed. With the editing complete, galley proofs approved, "T's" crossed and "I's" dotted, *Perfect* was perfect. I gave a final once-over and sent it to the printer. I planned book signings and scheduled meet-the-author events. There were women's conferences, and radio interviews. I was living out my dream. I pinched myself repeatedly to be sure it was real. My "ouch" was all the proof I needed to reassure me this *was* as good as it gets. Little did I know, while I was soaking up life and living the dream, storms were brewing off the coast of Paradise.

First, there was Tropical Depression Economy. It was stalled over Martin County for nearly a year producing low real estate values and high unemployment which contributed to my partner's unsuccessful job search. The highs and lows left heavy gray thunderclouds and increased atmospheric pressure in our home.

Then the hurricanes came. There was John, my patriarch storm in New Jersey. With gale force winds for eighty-one years dad weakened almost overnight. Drowning in himself, he held on to every ounce of power he could muster in his now fragile frame. He had barely begun to build strength when Hurricane Madeline, his companion storm for sixty years, spun over him and set down in a hospital nearly ten miles away. I immediately left the tropical depression in Florida and headed straight into the eye of the storm in New Jersey.

The skies cleared slowly. As they did, the economy brightened ... for me ... in New Jersey. I checked the extended forecast in both regions. The economic climate was better in New Jersey and both hurricanes had lost massive amounts of strength. They needed help ... lots of help. I put my writing dream on hold and tended to the needs of the moment. I cared for them. Work was a must. Bills needed to be paid. I added full-time bread winner to my already full plate of full-time caregiver. To keep the home fires burning, I made monthly weekend trips back to Florida.

Then the Tsunami hit. The wave sucked me in and pulled me deep into the undertow. "I need to be alone," was all he said. I spun, face down to the ocean floor and lay there dormant for months until I drifted ever so slowly to the surface. At the top, life came full circle. Both hurricanes stood strong on either side of me and I was surrounded by a rainbow of friends.

I spent today at Hole in the Wall working on my next novel, *Between the Devil and the Deep Blue Sea...* reaching for the brass ring.

Life can change as quickly as the weather, but if we never head into a storm, we may never see a rainbow.

Reach for the brass ring.
Treasure the people you love.
Honor those who love you.
Take care of yourself.
When you're down, look up.

"The need for change bulldozed a road down the center of my mind."

Maya Angelou

How far is Pluto?

Paulette Costa

Life is good. My closest circle knows the story of my life, specifically 2005 – 2011. For those who do not, suffice to say I was in the best and the worst places of my life during that time. I spent three years with the people who brought me into this world, watching one of them slowly slip away and though I didn't want to be in that geographical place, the experience was most rewarding … one I will carry with me the rest of my days. In addition to family time and totally unrelated to it, a sweet relationship came to a bitter end. I protected my heart for the next four years while it mended.

I decided it was time to move forward … but how? Friends had talked about online dating sites and dear friends had even found true love through one of them. I had tried online dating in 2003 when online dating wasn't cool, but it seems now to be the new substitute to the bar scene which pretty much stinks no matter what generation you are. It did seem a good enough way to weed out weirdoes (pardon me weirdoes), remain somewhat invisible, and possibly meet and make a few new friends. With those expectations, I bit the bullet, entered my information, uploaded pictures and waited.

I guess there really are plenty of fish in the sea. In two days, more than two hundred people had viewed my profile. My inbox filled ... a wink here, a flirt there, an actual composed message every now and then. For the most part I didn't see anything different in the online dating scene from 2003 to 2011 with the exception of receding hairlines and beer bellies. Okay, so I'm exaggerating ... a little ... very little.

My rule was easy: When a message arrives, check the sender's profile *first*, then decide my response ... no picture or no personal message equals no response. That narrowed the field tremendously. Hey, a girl has to have some standard especially when the field is pretty much invisible and when the girl is a huge Criminal Minds fan. Standards and all, I did meet a selective few very nice men. We shared stories and laughs over coffee and cocktails and went our separate ways.

I don't know what made me do it ... perhaps it was fate. ..

I clicked on a message one day before I checked the profile. It was short and sweet – a compliment and a comment that it was too bad we lived so far apart which made it virtually impossible for us to meet. Curious now, I checked his profile and discovered less than sixty miles separated us. I responded with a humorous comment about the distance which I viewed as a short jaunt considering my life and career. A fun banter began. After a few days of messaging we decided to meet.

Ten days separated the decision from the meeting and technology kept us not only in communication but in learning mode as well ... likes, dislikes, families, friends, careers – all the things we usually learn about people *after* we meet them face to face.

A fond and very special friendship formed first through our chats, conversations and pictures. I teased him one day and asked if Niantic was too far a drive to meet. He responded, "I'd go to Pluto to meet you!"

I waited patiently on a bench at Hole-In-The-Wall Beach. I brought a companion book along. My gaze shifted from my book to the water, but never to my right. I knew he would appear from that direction – one way in, one way out. Concentration eluded me. I kept my gaze down. People came and went, some sat on the bench alongside mine. We exchanged pleasantries while I wished them along their merry ways in my head.

I listened ... soft footsteps echoed through the tunnel ... I felt his approach. The breeze picked up, I lifted my eyes and looked into his. He had me from hello.

The only limits we have are the ones we put on

ourselves. Follow your dreams, even if they take you to Pluto. We can protect ourselves from pain forever. The downside to that is we also deny ourselves the joy waiting on the other side.

Invictus

Out of the night that covers me,
Black as the Pit from pole to pole,
I thank whatever gods may be
For my unconquerable soul.

In the fell clutch of circumstance
I have not winced nor cried aloud.
Under the bludgeonings of chance
My head is bloody, but unbowed.

Beyond this place of wrath and tears
Looms but the Horror of the shade,
And yet the menace of the years
Finds, and shall find, me unafraid.

It matters not how strait the gate,
How charged with punishments the scroll.
I am the master of my fate:
I am the captain of my soul.
William Ernest Henley

Paulette Costa

Paulette Costa is a life empowerment coach, mentor, business development consultant, writer and speaker. She can find a story in the simplest of situations. She is dynamic, always changing and growing. Her ability to adapt, grow and change will keep her in the forefront of authors and presenters who help us understand ourselves, what drives us, what we love and what we fear.

With wit and a down-to-earth approach, Paulette's writing and seminars are entertaining and inspiring. Her writing helps us make sense of our personal conflicts and she inspires people to look at the brighter side of life, think objectively through turmoil and stress, and grow from every experience.

Paulette Costa's published works include *Perfect*, a novel of self discovery as well as contributions to inspirational books, *Vibrant Women's Wisdom, Surviving and Thriving through Dark and Bright Hours* and *The Gratitude Project: Celebrating 365 Days of Gratitude*. These early works were published under the pseudonym PC McCullough. Newer works published are *Paulette Costa's Balancing Thoughts* and *Essential Empowerment: The Six Essential Elements to Creating and Living an Empowered Life.* Learn more about Paulette Costa and New Life Essentials at www.newlifeessentials.com

The turning point in the process of growing up is when you discover the core of strength within you that survives all hurt.

Max Lerner

God Is the Light I Follow

Julie Cox

When people see me with a huge smile on my face most of the time, they think my life is perpetually happy. Yes, my life is amazing, but it is far from perfect. God is still brewing me to perfection.

Ten years ago following surgery, I developed a chemical imbalance that impaired reasoning capabilities in my brain. It happened so quickly and I didn't realize what had hit me until I could no longer function. Nothing mattered. I was very depressed and angry with myself for feeling so grossly miserable every day.

My husband suffered with me, and together we decided I needed help. Counseling and medication were prescribed. Unfortunately, the medication had an adverse effect. I became suicidal and eventually hospitalized.

It was a defining moment for me. As always, I turned to prayer. The doctors explained that our brains are as much a part of our body as any part that gets sick or damaged and that I could pray all I wanted but only the right medication would help my brain heal and function properly. I listened to their advice and took my medication religiously.

During a four-year sabbatical in my homeland, the Philippines, I spent my time developing the property I had bought for my retirement. There I found the passion of my heart. I gardened from the first burst of sunlight to dusk, and at night I watched the birds fly in the pale moonlight. I found my heaven on earth, and most of all, I found my true self. I am not dead; I am so alive!

I found my peace and my inner strength again. I found God, the Light I follow. I found the reason why these things happen. He wanted me to see what I was living for and my divine reason of existence. I needed to share my blessings with those unfortunate people around me. He broke me to see the needs of other less fortunate. He wanted me to see that there are other colors in the rainbow, and things of God are found in the road less traveled.

I needed to go back to the Philippines to share my gift of nature. I needed to invite the homeless children of Manila and have them camp at my resort every year. I needed to have the Youth for Christ Ministry camp and spread the gospel of the Lord. I needed to show people how one person can make a difference, one person at a time.

I thank God for my bipolar illness. It brought me closer to Him once again.

"We are not human beings having a spiritual experience.
We are spiritual beings having a human experience."

Pierre Teilhard de Chardin

Julie Cox

Julie Cox is a survivor. She lived at the garbage dump of the Subic Bay Naval Base in the Philippine Islands for two years. At the age of fifteen, she was raped and was also diagnosed with leukemia.

She was raped again at twenty-four and this time left for dead. She became pregnant as a result. Julie had the baby instead of an abortion, gave the baby up for adoption, and found that same baby fourteen years later.

Her father gambled away her family's land, but Julie got it back, and more land to boot, with pristine waters running through it.

Poverty, rape number one, leukemia, rape number

two—no problem. Julie is halfway to becoming a millionaire. She's well on the way to realizing all her dreams.

Julie believes "Even if you're broken, negative, bitter, depressed, outmanned, and outgunned, nothing can stop you from finding your destiny!"

You can read Julie's story in her memoir, *I Ordered My Life Yesterday,* available at Amazon.com.

"All the art of living lies in a fine mingling of letting go and holding on."

Henry Ellis

My Epiphany

Nancy R. Hooper

Jesus didn't take me. I mustn't be good enough.

I was a shy, very impressionable seven-year-old who had just made her First Communion. During the months of instruction leading up to it, Sister Irene told us about a young girl who made her First Communion many, many years ago. She was so in love with Jesus that she died on the spot after receiving the host. I knew the same would happen to me. It didn't. The message I got: I wasn't good enough.

As I grew older, I perceived the message repeated in most aspects of my life. "I'm not good enough" morphed into "I'm not good," and, finally, "I'm not a good person." I married; we had two daughters. Still the internal litany continued. To the "I'm not a good daughter" I added "I'm not a good wife"; "I'm not a good mother." I simply wasn't good enough, not even to like myself, although I couldn't admit that part to anyone, even myself.

In my early fifties, I knew the dark cloud that shrouded me my entire life was depression, often deep depression, but I couldn't do anything about it. The necessary struggle was beyond me.

Enter Michele, who recognized my mental state. Our brief, nice-to-know-you conversation had ended when she suddenly said, "By the way, you're a good person." She was the first to ever say that to me, and I didn't believe her.

Michele and I became close friends. We ended each visit or conversation with, "You're a good person." "And you are, too." At first, it was lip service on my part, but with time and repetition, I began to wonder, could she be right? The years of not being good enough had a strong hold over me, though.

It happened just like in it does in children's books: "And then one day," in the shower, I had my epiphany.

Hold on! I *am* a good person! I have been all along!

I couldn't stop saying it. "I *am* a good person! I *am* a good person!" I think I even shouted it.

I remember a slight snap in my brain just before it happened, then my brain felt lighter, sunnier even. The cloud was gone, and so, too, was the weight that bore down on me for what, once it was gone, seemed like my entire life. I felt lighter physically and mentally.

The best part? For the first time in my life, I like myself—the thinking, breathing entity who is Nancy. What an overwhelming sense of empowerment! Avenues

I previously wouldn't consider exploring because I wasn't good enough now entice me with their possibilities. I now work to think in positives, stretching to improve this new, wonderful model of me.

Do I have bad days? Of course I do. But they're limited now, not infinite. The light and brightness of my future surround them. They will never totally control me again.

I *am* a good person!

"The mystery of life is not a problem to be solved but a reality to be experienced."

Art Van Der Leeuw

Nancy R. Hooper

Nancy Hooper has asked herself the tough questions all her life—the how's and the why's. She found some major answers when she had her epiphany.

Nancy started Hooper Editing Services in 1986 and has been in the editing field since 1972. She has two nonfiction reference books in the works, *Word Express*, a pocket grammar guide, and *Minutia for Classical Music Lovers—Factoids That Don't Appear in Program Notes.*

In her sparc time, Nancy reads and quilts. She lives in Connecticut with her husband and has two grown daughters.

"A man sooner or later discovers that he is the master-gardener of his soul, the director of his life."

James Allen

Out of the Darkness Comes the Light

Angie McDonald

"Out of the darkness comes the light" or so I had heard my entire childhood. The experience never made its way into my life; in fact, I had only encountered drama-filled obstacles because I was poor, fatherless and a product of the ghetto environment but no light, not even a spark… just drama-filled doom & gloom.

The day had finally come when I was the age I had dreamed of being. I was eighteen. I was also young and naïve but you couldn't tell *me* that. I had a job, a boyfriend, was out of school and looking toward the new beginning I would create for myself. The new chapter that would be so different than anything I had experienced my whole life. It was the summer of 1992 and I was thrilled.

I had not been feeling well but was not overly ill. Under my mother's expert and self-identified doctor's orders I decided to visit my physician. She examined me and told me she couldn't find anything wrong then asked if I had taken a pregnancy test. I thought she was stupid and probably looked at her that way too because she darted those "I know you're an active girl" eyes at me. I quickly put my head down and took a cab straight to the CVS. I rummaged through half a dozen boxes of "if it's an X, yes" or "pink and blue means who knows what" then finally picked the most expensive, reliable name brand test. I got home and was excited that my tribe of a family, mom, stepdad, four brothers and a sister were not home. I ran to the kitchen and downed an entire pitcher of iced tea then waited in the bathroom until I was ready to drown the toilet bowl. I read through the page filled with instructions on what and what not to do. I finally pulled the blue tape off and went for it.

An hour later I wanted to run away … far away. The darkness consumed me and I was suddenly afraid of my own shadow. I felt like I had let everyone down. I was the example in my home. The obedient student, smart with the potential to be the Spanish Barbara Walters, and I was eighteen and pregnant. What was I thinking and what would I tell my family, my mother who herself was a teenage mom and reminded me everyday how my life needed to be different. This would certainly disappoint her. I looked in the mirror and thought… "What a failure!" I hated myself and punched my stomach for what seemed like a million times over. I wanted this to not be true. I wanted to run until my feet bled, until my bones ached, until this baby was gone. I wanted it gone.

Three months later I finally found the nerve to confront my mother. She responded exactly how I imagined. She gave me the look I never wanted to see from her… disappointment. She ran through the various options she needed to but I had already made up my mind. I would sleep in the bed I had made. My mother did not speak to me until I was six months into my pregnancy. That was darkness like I had never known. I didn't know how to deal without her expert advice. The dark place I had placed myself in had zero light. I knew at that point people were full of shit. They make these statements without knowing what they speak just to sound good. Well I was living proof that when it is dark there is not light….

Eighteen years later, light fills my life. The crossroads which I call being a mother at a very young age came with so many pitfalls I needed to sprint over and I DID. On March 7, 1993 I gave birth to Gabrielle. Her name signifies the angel and she has been my angel, my light. She taught me how to love, how to live and how to find light in the darkest places. She taught me how to be a mother even at eighteen. It was not the end but just the beginning that I had been searching for all those years.

"It doesn't matter where you are, you are nowhere compared to where you can go."

Bob Proctor

Angelita McDonald

Angelita McDonald is the vice president of human resources for the Realogy Franchise Group at Realogy Corporation. Angelita leads the strategic development, talent attraction and implementation of human capital initiatives to align with overall business needs of the organization. She is a certified Professional in Human Resources and active member of SHRM.

Angelita currently resides in New Jersey with husband Richard and three children; Gabrielle, Lucas and Emilio. She is an avid reader and loves to write poetry and short stories. She is a certified Zumba instructor and looks to become more involved in Zumba training.

"It is better to conquer yourself than to win a thousand battles. Then the victory is yours. It cannot be taken from you, not by angels or by demons, heaven or hell."

Buddha

A Journey to Love

Paul Meijer

Life is a funny journey; forever changing. Sometimes you end up on roads you really have no idea how you got there. Sometimes those roads lead to new discoveries, new awareness and experiences, some painful some happy.

It was a busy Saturday in July... There were more clients than sales reps at the dealership. People were leaving. With a few minutes between clients I rushed downstairs for a quick lunch. After only my second bite into a wonderful sandwich my manager poked his head through the door and said; "I need you upstairs, people are leaving." I left my lunch and headed to the showroom. There I saw John heading toward the front door at a good pace with an annoyed look on his face. Trailing some twenty paces behind and trying to catch up with him was his wife. I intercepted them, introduced myself and apologized for the wait. After a brief interview, a car was selected and we were on our test drive. She was in the driver's seat, he in the front passenger's and I rode in back.

During the ride I felt a distinct physiological reaction the likes of which I had never experienced before. It felt as though this woman was looking at me through the back of her head. I couldn't process the feeling nor did I understand it at the moment though it had a profound effect on me. I wondered, "Exactly what is this feeling I have in my body right now?"

That feeling stayed with me for a few days when I received the first email. It was innocent enough ... a joke forward like one a friend would send. The email was followed up by a phone call, and another and another.

Winter approached. It was time for her yearly pilgrimage to Florida. An initial phone call from her turned into twenty-two hundred minutes in one month. I know this because it was when I got my first six hundred dollar phone bill.

When she returned we met for lunch and spent afternoons together. We could talk about anything at any time and those conversations would go on for hours. I was drawn to her. She made me feel like I had never felt before. I didn't realize it at the time but I was falling in love with her. Maybe I fell in love with her that afternoon in the car. I don't know... It *was* an amazing connection then and grew stronger as time progressed. We only wanted to spend more and more time together. It was the strongest connection I had ever felt toward a woman. I didn't even have those feelings for my wife to whom I was married twenty years. *That* was a series of "things I was supposed to do".

One Christmas Eve, she called me. We had a very long and intimate conversation. Unbeknownst to us, John had eavesdropped on the entire conversation. The shit hit the fan but I was relieved. I believed his permission opened the door for us to finally be together. I would no longer be the man in the shadows. I was ready to openly declare my feelings for her and share our lives together. I would go anywhere or do anything to make that happen. That was when she broke my heart. She said she would not leave John. "I would lose my kids, my grand kids, my friends. The world as I know it would come to an end."

"Then we can't continue this," I responded.

All my hopes and desires suddenly crashed around me. For weeks I lay in bed in the fetal position. I cried myself to sleep. I couldn't eat. There were days I had to leave work as I could not function. It was a world of tremendous joys followed by a profound sadness and depression that would be one of the darker periods of my life. I didn't want to meet anyone and I didn't want to do anything.

Many thirty-dollar co-pays later I decided that I had suffered enough. I lifted the veil of sadness that had covered my existence and moved on. If I learned only one thing from that love, it was that I wanted to love that way again.

And then it happened... nearly three years later on a dating website. The newest members popped up on the screen for all to see. There she was – one of the most beautiful women I had ever seen. *"Wow"* was my first reaction. I clicked on her profile to discover that she lived an hour away from me. Most my adult life I had lived by the twenty- minute rule. If I couldn't get somewhere within twenty minutes I wouldn't go. Certainly the prospect of meeting a woman who might as well have lived on Pluto did not appeal to me. I sent her a note stating I was sorry she lived so far away but that she was so beautiful I just had to write. That message started email banter back and forth which turned to a phone call that would forever change my life. I felt a connection from the first email and when I heard her voice on the phone that first time, electricity ran through my veins once again.

I decided to take the drive to meet her. She was a romantic just like me and pix messages leading to our meeting place kept ringing on my phone step-by-step until I received a picture of the park bench where she would be waiting for me.

As I came around the corner I saw the most beautiful woman wearing a blue dress. She was everything and more than I had hoped she would be. We had made a plan to cook dinner together and as we drove to the grocery store we held hands. Listening to my favorite Streisand album, Barbara sang the words; "Just when you thought love had passed you by, there you were." We clutched hands and cried together. I knew instantly she was the woman for me. I would marry her one day and be with her for the rest of my life.

Two months later we were engaged and are now planning our future together.

My former love, the disappointment that followed, and my determination to move forward taught me there is someone for each of us if we are open to love and *let* it happen. Things in life happen the way they are supposed to and at the time they are supposed to. I spent many years in a marriage filled with pain. So much so that the walls around my heart were steep. When we met, those walls lowered. I had no control over them.

People come in and out of each other's lives for specific reason and purpose. I believe that first love was brought into my life to show me what love is and that it could really happen if I let it. It taught me that one day love would come and it set me on a quest to find it. Knowing it existed ... out there ... somewhere ... made me want to find it again ... I did; this time though, with someone who loves me back with the same depth and emotion I have for her.

Most people either don't or will never know the true meaning of love. It has transformed me into the man I am today. It has allowed me to open up my heart and to find my soul mate… Paulette.

The beginning…

The Serenity Prayer

God grant me the serenity
to accept the things I cannot change;
courage to change the things I can;
and wisdom to know the difference.
Living one day at a time;
Enjoying one moment at a time;
Accepting hardships as the pathway to peace;
Taking, as He did, this sinful world
as it is, not as I would have it;
Trusting that He will make all things right
if I surrender to His Will;
That I may be reasonably happy in this life
and supremely happy with Him
Forever in the next.
Amen.
--Reinhold Niebuhr

Paul Meijer

Paul Meijer emigrated from Curacao to the United States when he was eight years old. A modern-day Renaissance man, his talents include gourmet cooking, cake decorating, building computers and home improvement contracting.

Paul has a passion and zest for life and has always been driven to be the best he can be. "Do for others with no expectation of anything in return and the laws of attraction will bring all good things to you." That is Paul's philosophy and it has served him well. In his thirty years in sales and management, he has repeatedly been recognized nationally for his commitment to providing outstanding customer service.

Of all his achievements, Paul is most proud of his daughters, Erika and Caroline.

"If you don't like something, change it. If you can't change it, change your attitude."

Maya Angelou

Moving to My Next Square
Casey Morley

I wondered how one could reach the age of thirty-five and not know he or she was part of a group. That was my experience one evening as I sat in a group therapy session and heard the word "dysfunctional." I remember thinking, what is that, and told myself to look up the word when I got home. As I read the definition, I suddenly got a sick feeling in my stomach–the reality of learning that I had come from a dysfunctional home and then, hours later, the realization that my boyfriend of five years had as well.

Quickly I learned he wanted nothing to do with this new awareness of mine. Even faster I learned a therapy session or two was not going to fix what is. I remember feeling as if I had received a diagnosis of cancer. I was devastated. What was more important, I was alone once again in life to deal with a situation bigger than me, bigger than life.

I know today what a blessing it is that awareness and healing come in stages, like peeling an onion. Otherwise, I could not have coped with what was in store for me on my journey of crawling out. I could not have handled having my trusted dirty old blanket of shame, guilt, fear, and denial pulled from me all at once.

The years of unveiling my true self one new awareness at a time was one of the hardest jobs I ever took on, almost as hard as being a single parent for the last eighteen years. The one step or one hour at a time made me look at life a little differently. I started to see myself as just standing on another square.

What I mean by another square is that, a while back, I started to see decision making as standing on a square. I learned to stop a minute, even 30 seconds, to ask myself, If I am standing on this square and I decide to do this or that, will I be going forward? Will I be going backwards? Will I be only side-stepping or standing still by deciding nothing for the moment? Taking that little bit of time to think helped tremendously. Going backwards was just not for me.

On this journey of mine, I was told many times by Dr. Amy, the woman who diagnosed me with post-traumatic stress disorder (PTSD), that women who have endured all that I have often end up institutionalized, or are addicts, or commit suicide. I have overcome huge obstacles and beat the odds on many levels. Her words "always remember what an incredibly strong woman you are" continue to empower me on the tough days.

What I do know better than my own name is that I broke the cycle. I broke the cycle of generation after generation raising dysfunctional children in dysfunctional homes. My son may have grown up with only one parent, but he knows what a home filled with unconditional love looks and feels like. And, yes, I do believe he will raise the first functional family in our family tree. I gave him the birthright we were all put on this earth to have.

"Most of the important things in the world have been accomplished by people who have kept on trying when there seemed to be no hope at all."

Dale Carnegie

Casey Morley

Casey Morley has worked throughout her adult life to emerge from and come to terms with a life filled with every form of abuse. She chronicles her journey in her book *Crawling Out*.

Casey is a lifelong resident of Connecticut and a single mother to a wonderful eighteen-year-old son, Michael. She has enjoyed working in the beauty industry for forty years, the last twenty as the owner of her own business.

For fun, she loves to cook and entertain her legion of friends in her welcoming loving home.

"You must be the change you wish to see in the world."

Mohandas Gandhi

Life is a Path

Patricia Nealon

Things were going along just fine, just as I thought they would. After all I was a good kid. I studied hard; got straight A's and excelled in college. I landed a great job and married a 'prince'. Not bad for a gal from the Bronx.

Life was super: moved to the burbs, bought a house, found a puppy and got two kids. Everything was moving along just as I had planned; moved to a bigger house, got a bigger dog, found a better job, my prince got promoted … just as I had planned.

Hey well what's this? All of a sudden my life seems to be crumbling apart. I was in New York City on 9/11, a loved one passes away, and kids are getting in trouble at school. What happened to all my planning? Well don't worry, I tell myself, things will get better and back on plan.

Heck what's happening to me? Things are getting

worse. Son gets in trouble at school and gets kicked out, I lose my job, the dog runs away, a tree falls on the house. This is not going according to plan. Well don't worry, I tell myself, things will get better and back on track.

I can't believe it. Things are getting worse. Son in trouble again and gets kicked out of his new school, I get a new job then lose the job, the house gets flooded, *and* my best friend moves away. Well don't worry. I can fix everything and get things to work according to plan.

Things are getting even worse. My prince loses his job, the car is totally destroyed in an accident, suicidal threats, son is on drugs, we lose the house and have no health insurance, but not to worry, things can't get worse - I can handle this all according to my plan.

Can things get any worse? Unfortunately yes. No jobs, no cash, lose pension, son in trouble, can't purchase medicines or medical insurance. My plan no longer works.

How about that? My plan doesn't work. Guess what I just found out. I am not in control. I can't make things work by studying hard, by controlling or by wishing and praying. I can't make things happen. I am not in control. I can't do it by myself.

Is this some secret everyone else knows except me? What a relief! I am not in control. Guess what! I don't have to worry about anything anymore because I am not in control.

Yesterday happened.

I can't change it.

I can't worry about it.

It is G O N E.

It doesn't really make a difference now.

Tomorrow isn't here.

I can't worry about *it*.

I have no control over it anyway.

There is only today, and I am not in control.

I am F R E E!

Here's the secret: God is in control. If you don't believe in God then the secret is: there is some plan for each of us. The point is: each of us must take our own path. Life *is* its own path.

"Life's challenges are not supposed to paralyze you, they're supposed to help you discover who you are."

Bernice Johnson Reagon

Patricia Nealon

Patricia lives in Connecticut with her husband and two adopted sons from Guatemala. She was raised in the Bronx and her education includes a BS degree in Family and Consumer Studies from Lehman College and a MBA and Post Master's Certificate in Accounting and Finance from Iona College. Patricia worked at JP Morgan Chase for over twenty-two years mainly as a Financial Manager in operations. Upon leaving the bank Patricia worked for a small money management company. She was the controller for a nursery school in Scarsdale, New York. She now works as the Business Manager at the Clelian Center a ministry of the Apostles of the Sacred Heart.

Patricia volunteers her accounting services as the treasurer in the Franciscan Family Apostolate and she is in the Secular Franciscan Order. She is a black belt in Taekwondo.

"Follow your honest convictions, and stay strong."

William Thackeray

Embracing Change
Delores M. Rubino

The year is 1998 and after twenty-two years and the births of eight children, I will be divorced by June. Six children will remain at home, ranging in age from two to sixteen years. I know this man will not be a faithful provider after the divorce; he has not been able to fill that role in the marriage. What are my options? Certainly not to continue receiving state assistance.... this is not acceptable to me any longer. *Think, Delores, think. Consider your current assets and abilities.*

The divorce, in itself a life changer, would set into motion the biggest turning point of my life. I decided to build on my undergraduate degree and former teaching experience by applying to the University of Oregon Masters Program for Early Intervention/Early Childhood Special Education. My five year old son was born with Down syndrome and had already received early intervention services. I was intensely interested and knew I had the skills to do this work for other hurting families. The time to pursue this passion was now.

In September of 1999 I found myself on campus, studying alongside fellow students, all of whom were quite a bit younger than I. At forty-nine years old, I was the elder stateswoman of the group as well as the only mom of a child with a disability. Both unique positions worked to my advantage. All my life experience had laid the groundwork, the yellow brick road, for my successful completion of the program. One year later, in August of 2000, I walked with my classmates as a graduate while my family beamed and celebrated my achievement. I began working in the field one month later. My earning potential was increased to make caring for my growing family possible. We moved into the home I currently own and found a stability we had not ever experienced.

Proud? You bet. And looking back now, I know the day I met with the department head at the University was possibly the most significant TURNING POINT in my life. Her words of encouragement nudged my ruby slippers in the direction of OZ: "Delores, we love to have parents of children with special needs apply to the program. We find they have the heart for this work. Your experiences raising a child who has Down syndrome have already prepared you. We would love to have you join us. You can do this." I embraced those words and have never looked back.

"Never be satisfied with what you achieve, because it all pales in comparison with what you are capable of doing in the future."

Rabbi Nochem Kaplan

Delores M. Rubino

Delores, mother of eight amazing children, has been a single mom since 1998, when her marriage of twenty-two years ended in divorce. She currently works as an Autism Consultant, supporting teaching staff, conducting parent trainings, and teaching children between two and five years of age.

A baby boomer in the process of reinvention, Delores is finding new avenues of self-expression through blogging and speaking. She endeavors to shower those she meets with refreshing encouragement, self-confidence, and hope. A cheerleader at heart, Delores uses enthusiasm and humor to support her listeners.

Visit her website: www.stateofdelorium.com, and fan page, State of Delorium on Facebook.

"Change is the law of life. And those who look only to the past or present are certain to miss the future."

John F. Kennedy

Are You Talking to Me?
Ann Volpe Sack

I had known Joe for just a short time, yet after a day of starched business meetings we struck up a conversation about our in-born gifts. I admitted that art was my greatest passion, but I had largely abandoned it since college to focus on work and real life. "I hate it when people have talent and don't use it," he said sharply. His comment smacked me squarely on the forehead and reverberated throughout my body. "Why aren't you using your talent?" it echoed. My artistic self had been pleading for resurrection for some time, but after absorbing his terse statement, I could no longer ignore it.

Although drawing and painting came naturally since I was a child, making art after a long absence seemed impossible. I was rusty, I didn't know where to begin, and I had laundry to do.

At the time, the art world extolled the virtues of abstract works and expression for expression's sake. With a personal bent toward realism, I wondered if I'd been born at the wrong time or on the wrong planet. Why would I bother to draw trees when others were exploring the profundities of life? Nonetheless, I began a circuitous quest.

Despite persistent doubts, I regularly visited the art materials at the local craft store. They were beautiful, colorful and alive, and being surrounded by them was sustaining. I studied the subtle variations in color in the tubes of paint. I smelled the graphite pencils, felt the textures of the colored papers, and imagined making highly flourished letters with the calligraphy sets. As I scanned the shelves I envisioned a thousand possibilities, but they were all unreachable. At the end of each visit, I walked back to my car empty handed.

Finally on a pivotal day, I picked up three bottles of shoe paint and a paint brush and carried them to the check-out counter, out to my car, and then home.

I brought out my black flats which were still in good condition. The seams in the leather divided the shoes into varied sections, so I painted them alternately with turquoise, fuchsia and black.

I was thrilled with the results. Colorful shoes were all the rage, but I had designed that pair myself. More importantly, the feeling of holding a paint brush was indescribable. Within minutes, it seemed unnatural to be without one, as if a lost part of my anatomy had returned to its rightful place.

I painted more shoes and then progressed to other projects. Most were outside the realm of fine art, but they helped build my confidence. Ultimately, they led to my next leap of faith.

All my art supplies from college were in one drawer. I ventured in one day, pulled out a graphite pencil and began to draw. The sketches were simple and unrefined, yet the practice was transforming. It brought me back to the experience that was most familiar and most natural, and it gave me courage to do more. Since then, art has returned to its rightful place in my life.

If not for my persistent inner voice and Joe's directive, I might have lost touch with my innate forms of expression. I am grateful for the events that gave rise to an authentic and enlightening journey.

"We would accomplish many more things if we did not think of them as impossible."

C. Malesherbes

Ann Volpe Sack

Ann believes strongly in the transformative power of creative expression and in the value of every human voice. Among her goals is the desire to encourage artists – women in particular - to speak, write and create without limitations.

As a fine artist, her preferred mediums are graphite and colored pencils, and oils; her favored subjects are florals and still lifes. She is also a graphic designer and the proprietor of Ann Sack Design in Farmington, Connecticut, where she works primarily with corporate clients. She can be contacted at a.sack@comcast.net.

"For the past 33 years, I have looked in the mirror every morning and asked myself: 'If today were the last day of my life, would I want to do what I am about to do today?' And whenever the answer has been 'No' for too many days in a row, I know I need to change something."

Steve Jobs

Being Mrs. Right

Linda Wiggins

I'm not sure when I first noticed it. My ability to get a guy to fall for me seemed to vanish. Around age twenty-nine, I decided I wanted to get married and have a family of my own. My approach was to dazzle a guy and then move fast to show him how great a catch I'd be. It was always so great in the beginning, before I cared much about a man. Once I decided to pursue the relationship, however, the man lost interest and I crashed and burned.

I grew up in the 1960s and '70s, when it became passé to wait for a man to do the pursuing. Women's liberation. Civil rights. We could do anything, and now the "we" included women. I became the first in my Detroit-based family to get a college degree, so I soaked up more notions from university culture about the "failed" patriarchal system. Additional years as a reporter in newsrooms across the country pumped into my head that white males are as suspect as God and Jesus Christ. Maybe I was simply absent the day they handed out relationship skills.

Upon hearing yet another vitriol of a date gone wrong, a friend asked if I thought I had a problem with relationships and handed me a book on romance addiction. It hit the nail on the head and I soon devoured every book I could get my hands on that had to do with codependency and how to have healthy relationships. I can't tell you how many times and in how many forms I read, "Before someone else can love you, you first have to love yourself."

Nothing I read could teach me HOW to do this, until I came across the very practical book, *Mars and Venus on a Date* by Dr. John Gray of *Men are from Mars, Women are from Venus* fame. I no longer had to wait until I valued myself enough for it to resonate with potential love interests. Whatever the cause for my inability to create a sustained, loving relationship, there came a time I stopped trying to figure it out because there was never any cheese at the end of that tunnel.

Gray taught me that while the times had changed, men and women had not. Men still needed to be the pursuers, and women needed to show appreciation of men for their efforts to please us. I learned how to make my needs known in a way that motivated a man to meet them, and to return the favor not with what I might need, but what a man truly needs.

That was my Turning Point. When the pain of operating my old way became greater than the discomfort of change, I finally was able to operate in this new way, what I believe is God's way, and leave my way, or the way of the world, behind. I learned that it was not about finding Mr. Right, but first *Being Mrs. Right*.

"You have a very powerful mind that can make anything happen as long as you keep yourself centered."

Dr. Wayne W. Dyer

Linda Wiggins

Linda Wiggins is a writer and community leader living in Melbourne, Fla., with her husband and two children. She founded the nonprofit RelatioNSync in 2009 out of her passion to make available to others that which she was given, a chance to have a family of her own. She overcame obstacles to earn a college degree and earn a living in journalism. After realizing she wanted a family of her own at age 30, it became clear that her approach to dating would only continue to bring drama and pain. She blazed an eight-year path consuming relationship education in the form of books, workshops and coaching until she realized "It's not about Finding Mr. Right, but first Being

Mrs. Right," her theme for giving back to women who discover that the tools to success in the workplace do not necessarily produce victory in love. Linda realized that disadvantaged populations needed this intervention the most, and we as a community could not afford for them not to have it. RelatioNSync exists to bring healthy dating, marriage strengthening, positive parenting and workplace success skills to those who need it and cannot afford it. Linda can be reached at LindaWiggins123@aol.com.

"Happiness is not something you postpone for the future; it is something you design for the present."

Jim Rohn

Reader's Resources

Recognizing Turning Points...
How will I know?

Turning points occur when we least expect them and often when we are least ready for them. Mostly though, turning points occur when we most *need* them. By simply being aware you can change your life for the better.

Were you profoundly affected by a recent experience or event?

Turning points are personal, therefore, not necessarily profound events but events that have profound effect on an individual and that cause the individual to see some "thing" differently.

What's going on in your gut?

I once heard a speaker use the term "gut meter" to help participants recognize the importance of paying attention to all the signals for change. It is usually when our gut meter goes way to the far side we know change in our lives is eminent.

Do you anticipate the experience will make you a different person or make your life different?

Turning points can include life-altering decisions. You can quit smoking cold turkey or commit to complete a degree study.

How are you responding to what you experienced?

Sometimes we turn on a dime, other times more slowly. Similarly some events have an immediate impact on our lives while others manifest themselves quietly in our soul and though the change is not immediate, it is nonetheless impactful when it occurs.

How far outside your comfort zone are you?

It is easy to become comfortable with a discomfort in our lives believing if we don't change anything, we at least know the devil we face. In order to change, we must step outside our comfort zone. It is only when face a situation head on that we can resolve it.

Suggested Reading

<u>Transitions</u> - Julia Cameron (Prayers and Declarations for a Changing Life) Copyright 1999, Jeremy P. Tarcher/Putnam, New York

<u>The Power of Experience</u> - Edited by Jeremy Janes, Introduction by Gail Sheehy (Great Writers over 50 on the Quest for a Lifetime of Meaning) Copyright 2007, Sterling Publishing Co., Inc. for AARP, New York

<u>God on a Harley</u> - Joan Brady, Copyright 1995, Pocket Books of Simon & Schuster, Inc.

<u>The Prophet</u>- Kahlil Gibran, Copyright 1923, Alfred A. Knopf, New York

<u>The Velveteen Principles: a Guide to Becoming Real</u> - Toni Raiten-D'Antonio Copyright 2004, Health Communications, Inc., Deerfield Beach, FL

<u>More Notes From the Universe: Life, Dreams, and Happiness</u> - Mike Dooley Copyright 2005, 2008,

Atria Books (Simon & Schuster) New York/Beyond Words Publishing, Hillsboro, Oregon

Why Is God Laughing? The Path to Joy and Spiritual Optimism- Deepak Chopra Copyright 2008 Harmony Books, New York

Anam Cara A Book of Celtic Wisdom - John O'Donohue Copyright 1997, HarperCollins Publishers, New York

The Dance: Moving to the Rhythms of Your True Self - Oriah Mountain Dreamer Copyright 2001, HarperSanFrancisco a division of HarperCollins Publishers

Balancing Thoughts – Paulette Costa Copyright 2011, New Life Essentials LLC

Feel The Fear and Do It Anyway – Susan Jeffers, PhD. Copyright 1978, Random House Publishing Group

The Secret – Rhonda Byrne Copyright 2006, Atria Books/Beyond Words Publishing

My Turning Points Notes

My Turning Points Notes

My Turning Points Notes